Jo Foster has been fascinated by history since she discovered that life hadn't always been like it was in 1980s Essex. Since studying history at university, she has made a living working in TV, researching programmes including *The Worst Jobs in History*, *Time Team* and *Who Do You Think You Are?*

If I was a kid with a time machine, I'd want Jo Foster to be my guide. She has an insatiable historical curiosity, treats both the past and the present with verve and gusto and has a mischievous sense of humour that would keep me smiling throughout my journey

D1350228

The Great
Exhibition Mission

HISTORY
SPIES

JO FOSTER

ILLUSTRATED BY SCOULAR ANDERSON

MACMILLAN CHILDREN'S BOOKS

First published 2009 by Macmillan Children's Books
a division of Macmillan Publishers Limited
20 New Wharf Road, London N1 9RR
Basingstoke and Oxford
Associated companies throughout the world
www.panmacmillan.com

ISBN 978-0-330-44901-4

3 5 7 9 8 6 4 2

A CIP catalogue record for this book is available from the British Library.

Typeset by Perfect Bound Ltd
Printed and bound in the UK by CPI Mackays, Chatham ME5 8TD

The Publisher would like to thank the following for permission to reproduce
their material. Every care has been taken to trace copyright holders. However, if
there have been unintentional omissions or failure to trace copyright holders, we
apologise and will, if informed, endeavour to make corrections in any future edition.

Pages 31 Getty Images/Hulton Archive; 38 Alamy/Mary Evans Picture Library;
46 Alamy/Mary Evans Picture Library; 50 Mary Evans Picture Library;
57 Mary Evans Picture Library; 89 Alamy/Mary Evans Picture Library

Once upon a time, my life was almost as boring as yours.

Then on my birthday last year, I got a phone call: it was a bloke from the Department for Historical Accuracy. See, the government have invented a way to travel back in time. They wanted someone to travel around and check up on what really happened in history. And they picked me. Probably because of my astounding talents and unusually large brain, I expect. Since then, I've been travelling through time spying on the craziest stuff. Battles and magicians and feasts and duels. All sorts!

And now you're coming along too, and you're with the best guide around. I'll make sure you get to see everything that's worth seeing!

I'll show you what to wear, what to eat, where to go, how people have fun, where they live – everything. Stick with me and almost nothing can go wrong.

Department for Historical Accuracy

HISTORY SPY 00001
NAME CHARLIE CARTWRIGHT
CLEARANCE ULTRA

Pass must be carried at all times when on official missions. Not valid without stamp.

HISTORY SPIES

Our next top-secret History Spy mission is to...

ENGLAND
LONDON
1851

If you want to be a History Spy, you have to keep secrets. You have to keep your eyes open all the time, and remember everything, and most of all you have to be invisible. I don't mean like magic-cloak invisible. The best way to be invisible is to look just like everyone else.

Different times always need a different look, even in the same year. See, you could do something in December and look totally normal:

But if you tried it in July, everyone would stare.

Got the idea? Good.
But before we go, there
are a few things we'd
better get straight.

Dapper Disguises

1851 is a great time for dressing up. Er, sorry, I mean it's a great time for spies like us to put together a disguise to blend into the crowd. Firstly, there are loads of places to get hold of all kinds of clothes. I found most of these in Petticoat Lane market in East London. You can buy all kinds of secondhand clothes there. You'd stand out if you wore brand new clothes, because most people can't afford them.

The other reason I like 1851 disguises is that they're totally crazy. And Londoners have the silliest clothes of all. Try some of these for size:

Long scarf: popular for boys in chilly weather

Sailor suit: parents love dressing their kids in these.

I can't think of anything more embarrassing!

Gentlemen

Top hat: every chap's favourite headwear. If you're dressing as a gentleman, make sure it's black silk. All kinds of men can get away with a top hat in 1851, not just circus ringmasters. They're not really for kids though, and definitely not for ladies

Collar turned down over a big loose bowtie

Bright silk tie, gold tiepin

Embroidered shirt

Waistcoat: no smart gent should be without one, the brighter the better. Try canary-yellow silk or red velvet for a classy-looking belly

Frock coat: an outer layer for a chilly day

Tight checked trousers

Ankle boots

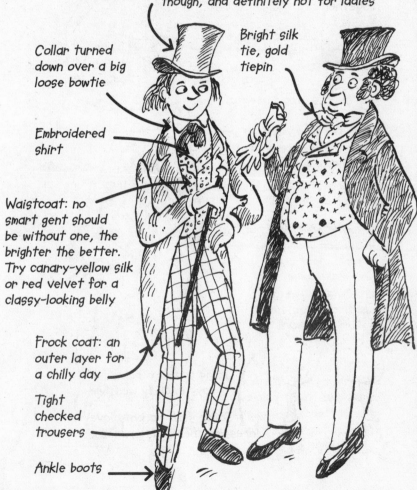

Ladies

Chemise: goes next to your skin, under your corset and petticoats

Corset: essential to give you the 'right' shape for 1851

Petticoats: you'll need at least five of them to bulk your skirt out, and to stop your knees from getting cold

Shawl: a holey knitted shawl for poor girls, a fancy soft one for posh ladies. Try crossing it over your chest and knotting it behind your back

Big frilly skirt: the more frills and bright colours, the better. Short skirts for girls, long ones for grown-ups

Ringlets: if you can't get your hair to curl, do it up. Centre partings are a must

Bonnet: flat back, flowers, ribbons

Tippet: short cape to wear outdoors in winter

Long 'drawers' (knickers): don't worry if these stick out of the bottom of your skirt, it's normal!

Footwear: dainty pumps for indoor use, practical boots for everyday use

Silk parasol: no one wants a tan in 1851. Not because it's bad for you, but because it looks 'common'. You can't buy SPF30 sunscreen, so for now, parasols will have to do instead

Fashion Victims

Female History Spies on assignment in 1851 will look a very strange shape if they don't wear a corset. They can be dangerous, though, and should be used with caution. Corsets squish your innards up and can make your spine bend in all the wrong places! And you don't get away with it just because you're a kid. Victorians give their daughters corsets when they're very young, and even make them wear corsets at night.

I am SO glad I'm not a girl. But if you think corsets sound ridiculous, wait until you see the crinoline. In a couple of years, everyone will be wearing them. They're supposed to help women get that 'jingle-bell' look without wearing so many layers and layers of heavy petticoats. You just wear a big birdcage under your skirt instead.

Carrying out missions while wearing a crinoline requires a great deal of practice. Even fitting through doors can be tricky. However, a crinoline can also be useful for a History Spy, as you can hide plenty of gadgets in it.

In 1885, a woman going by the name of Sarah Ann Henley will jump off the Clifton Suspension Bridge in Bristol. She'll survive the 76-metre drop when a gust of

Sorry, Miss, you'll have to leave yer crinoline outside.

Cartoon from Punch magazine, 1858

wind gets up her skirt and turns her crinoline into a parachute, so that she drifts gently back to the ground.

There is a rumour that this woman was a History Spy wearing a modified 'ejector crinoline'. The Department for Historical Accuracy has officially denied this.

One quick check before you go:

X NO jeans – they're invented for workmen in America in 1872.

X NO zips – don't wear these until the 1890s at the very earliest.

X NO trousers for girls – this would give people a terrible shock. To look normal round here, girls have to wear about ten skirts at the same time.

OK, so you look fine. But make sure you pay attention to the next bit – if you get any of this stuff wrong, we're bound to be found out. If anyone finds out about the History Spies we'll be in big trouble back home, as well as in 1851.

Vital Background Briefing

The essential quick-reference guide for History Spies completing missions in 1851. Keep this with you at all times.

London is the biggest city in the world, and it's growing fast. 1851 is the first year ever when more people in Britain live in towns than in the countryside, and London is the greatest of them all. It's still much smaller than in the twenty-first century, of course. Some places, like Peckham and Hammersmith, are still small towns outside London, in the countryside.

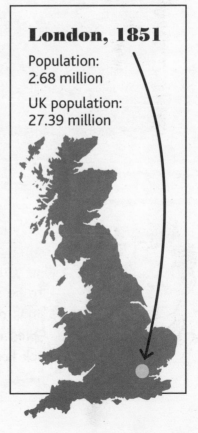

London, 1851

Population:
2.68 million

UK population:
27.39 million

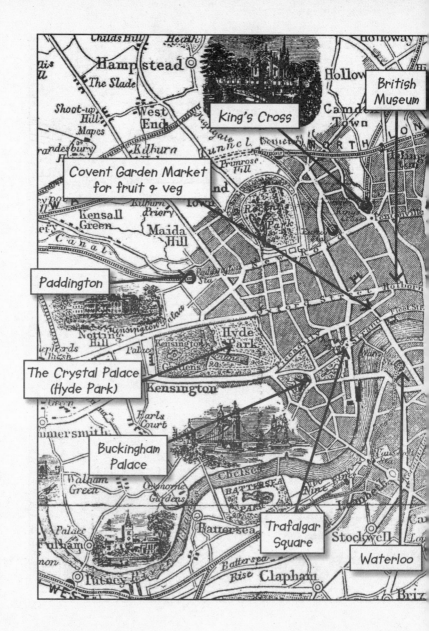

King's Cross

British Museum

Covent Garden Market for fruit & veg

Paddington

The Crystal Palace (Hyde Park)

Buckingham Palace

Trafalgar Square

Waterloo

14

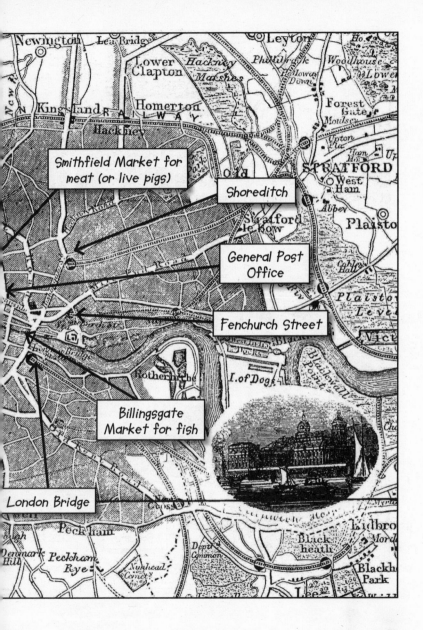

Smithfield Market for meat (or live pigs)

Shoreditch

General Post Office

Fenchurch Street

Billingsgate Market for fish

London Bridge

15

Getting Around

Travelling around the country is much quicker and easier in 1851 than it was even just a few years ago. Getting around may seem difficult to History Spies used to driving or cycling, but it could be much worse. Before the railways took over in the 1840s, you had to get in a stagecoach to go anywhere, which took ages.

I hate stagecoaches. They feel like you're being shaken around on a broken rollercoaster. If we ever go back to 1820 I'll show you.

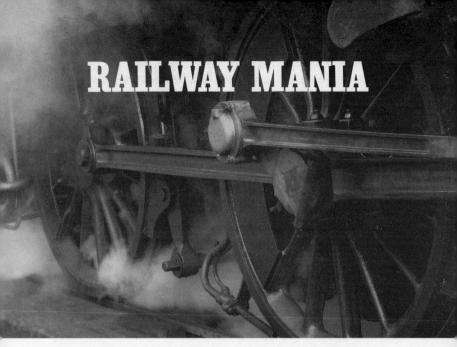

RAILWAY MANIA

The latest fashion fad that's sweeping the nation is ... trains. Yes, it's not geeky to be a trainspotter in 1851. Railways are a get-rich-quick scheme for anyone with a bit of money to spend. Over a few years in the 1840s, businessmen have spent so much money on building the railways that you can now get to pretty much any town in Britain by train. The whole country's changing, with new tunnels and massive bridges like the Forth Bridge.

Even the time of day is changing! Before the railways, every town in Britain could be in a slightly different time zone and it didn't matter. But the trains have to run on time everywhere. Soon, everyone is setting their clocks to 'Railway Time'.

Most people are terrified when they first see a train. They're huge, noisy and powerful, and they blow hot steam out of their engines like angry dragons. They go faster than anyone has ever travelled before. Doctors are warning that awful things can happen to your body if you travel at crazy speeds like 45mph. Watch out for the dreaded Railway Spine! If you're really nervous, you might want to visit one of the insurance offices at the train station. You can insure your life before you get on the train.

Actually, there *are* a lot of accidents on the railways, but they're not all train crashes. Some passengers get hurt because they don't realize how dangerous it is to get on or off when the train's still moving.

First class is for rich ladies and gentlemen, and you can even arrange to take your horse on the train if you're off hunting in the countryside.

Across Country

CANAL BOAT Used to move goods around. You can also go on them as a passenger. It's cheap, but it takes ages.

STEAM LAUNCHES Steam-powered boats, handy for day trips along the Thames or to the seaside at Margate.

Overseas
STEAMSHIPS

Iron steamships are crossing the oceans in 1851, taking people and goods all across the world. If you need to leave the country, you'll have to get a boat. They're much slower than planes of course – getting to America will take at least ten days, and sometimes a few weeks if the weather's bad.

Not Yet:

BICYCLES There aren't any bicycles until the middle of the 1860s. Some inventors are playing with the idea of the 'velocipede', which is like a bicycle without pedals that you push along with your feet. But mostly, until the 1860s, History Spies will just have to walk.

If you fancy having a go on one of these monsters, come back in the 1870s and try one of their bikes. It's the scariest ride I've ever been on. Once you've fallen off a few times you should start to get the hang of it!

The trick is to keep looking straight ahead, and to get off while you're still moving. If you try to stop before you get off, you fall off sideways.

THE UNDERGROUND Londoners don't have too long to wait for the Tube. In 1863 the Metropolitan Underground Railway will be opened, running from Paddington to Farringdon.

It's not really like the Tube in our time though. Think about it – a load of steam trains, in a tunnel. You can hardly breathe, what with that and the stinking gas lamps that don't really light the place up. It's like getting stuck down a coalmine full of chain-smokers. Bleurgh!

AEROPLANES It's annoying that it takes weeks to get to New York instead of seven hours, but if you want to travel by plane you'll have to wait until the twentieth century.

Quids In

Victorians use pounds and pence like we do back home. But they use a whole bunch of other coins too. And a pound isn't even 100 pence, it's 240! It makes sense to them, but I've never got it. See if you can work it out.

Victorian money is split into POUNDS (L), SHILLINGS (S) and PENCE (D). They're called 'L,S,D' not 'P,S,P' because the letters are short for the Latin coins *Libra*, *Solidus* and *Denarius*.

Got it yet? This simple table should clear things up.

	1 shilling (*s*)	=	12 pence (*d*)
1 pound (*l*) =	20 shillings (*s*)	=	240 pence (*d*)

This might not be too hard, if it really was that simple. But you won't just find three different coins in your pocket. As well as the pound (also called a sovereign), the shilling (also called a bob) and penny, you could come across the following coins: half sovereign (10s), crown (5s), half crown (2½s), florin (2s), sixpence, groat (4 pence), threepence, twopence, halfpenny, and farthing (¼ of a penny). At least you shouldn't have to worry about bank notes. There aren't many around in 1851.

However hard it seems, History Spies *must* make the effort to master Victorian money before travelling to 1851. Fumbling with money instantly makes a person stand out as foreign.

Lost in Translation

History Spies should watch their language at all times. Use this handy phrasebook to make sure you sound as Victorian as you look.

Bob – shilling

Cop – take or catch. A policeman can cop a thief, but don't call him a copper – yet.

Cove – man

Funk – either a bad smell or an attack of nervousness. Nothing to do with music or fashion, yet.

Half-a-bull – a half crown ($2\frac{1}{2}$ shillings)

Knocked up – tired, exhausted

Lush – a kind of alcoholic drink

Nosegay – bunch of flowers (see p. 100 for what they might mean)

Pal – friend, mate

Rookery – slum

Skyscraper – a slang nickname for a tall man or a tall hat. Skyscraper buildings don't exist yet.

Swell – a posh or well-dressed man

Tile – slang for a hat

Quid/bean/couter – £1

Quod – to put in prison

Velocipede – bicycle (though you're not likely to meet one – see p. 24)

Water closet/W.C. – loo. People won't understand you if you say loo, and if you ask for the toilet you'll be shown a room for getting dressed in.

So, how do you fancy a false identity? You might need to pick a fake name to travel back to 1851. Personally, I'm sticking with Charlie, but aliases can be fun.

Codename: Lettice

History Spies with modern names, such as Kylie or Dwight, should pick a Victorian alias to make undercover work easier. William and Mary are the most common names for boys and girls, and will fit with any kind of false identity.

If you fancy something flashier, though, try out some of these names:

Girls:

Charity   Lettice   Araminta
Winifred   Millicent
Adelaide   Ada   Fanny

Boys:

Bertram   Edwin   Albert
Ezekiel   Abel   Job
Waterhouse   Amos

Hmm ... Waterhouse Cartwright. I like it!

Take Me To Your Leader

History Spies File:
Queen Victoria Of Hanover

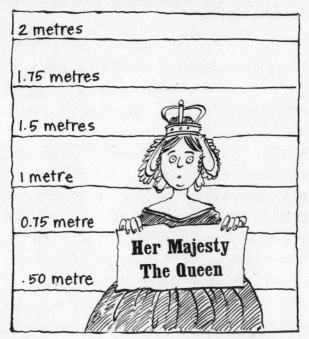

Born: 1819

Height: 4ft 11in (1.5 metres)

Hair: Brown

Distinguishing features: Crown

Age in 1851: 32 years

Eyes: Blue

Occupation: Queen

Victoria is married to the tall, handsome German Prince Albert. You probably know her as a short, fat woman in black who didn't have a sense of humour, but she only gets properly miserable after Albert dies.

In 1851 she's still a cheerful and loving wife, as well as the most important person in the whole of the British Empire. She likes her little dogs, music, opera and dancing. Also, she doesn't start wearing black until Albert dies. She's normally dressed in bright checks and stripes, and her favourite colour is parrot green.

She's very much in love with Albert and they have nine children together – it's all going well for them right now.

Victoria's a major celebrity, and places all over the world get named after her. This is partly because she rules for such a long time. She was crowned in 1837 and dies in 1901, meaning she gets to be Queen for a whopping 64 years. She makes cosy family life trendy, and she's keen on people being good and doing their duty. If she hadn't had kids, or if she'd been selfish and wanted to spend all her money on big parties, ice cream and hot-air balloons, maybe things would have been different.

> Maybe when you say Victorian you'd mean 'fun-loving and a bit silly' instead of 'strict and serious'.

The Long Arm of the Law

Watch out for policemen – here's a guide to spotting them.

There aren't proper police forces everywhere in the country yet. In London, though, the Metropolitan Police have been around for a while and they're pretty easy to spot.

While everyone's still working out what exactly a policeman's job is, you can use your local bobby as an alarm clock. Just go along to a police station, pay a few pence a week, and tell them what time you want an officer to come round and get you out of bed. Remember not to try this when you get back to your own time.

And don't forget: even though they double up as alarm clocks, policemen can still dish out some pretty horrible punishments if they catch you breaking the law.

In our time, people who leave Britain for Australia are usually looking for a better life in the sunshine – surfing, having barbecues and spotting kangaroos. In 1851, being sent to Australia is a terrible punishment. It's called 'transportation'. The journey takes months, and it's horrific.

Imposing height – Metropolitan Police officers have to be at least 5'8" (that's 1.73 metres) tall, which makes them bigger than most Victorians.

1: Top hat – makes him look stern, and helps him stand out in a crowd. It's also reinforced, to protect him from dings on the head.

2: Rattle – used before policemen got whistles, to call other policemen if he gets into trouble. Of course a radio would have been more use, but they don't exist yet.

3: Handcuffs – for apprehending naughty criminals

4: Tailcoat – to make him look like a servant, because he's supposed to serve the people

5: Truncheon – for the dishing out of wallops

6: Cutlass – He may look a bit silly, but don't get in the way of an 1851 policeman. He's armed to the teeth!

If you still think being sent to Australia sounds like a holiday, be warned: there are worse fates. Really bad crimes like murder, treason and piracy can get you a death sentence, usually by hanging in public.

But you can get punished for much smaller things in 1851 too. Kids get sent to prison for all kinds of daft things, from throwing stones to knocking on doors and running away.

Prisons are grim places where they make you do pointless work, like carrying cannonballs across a yard, or turning a handle on a box a certain number of times.

Don't worry. We are definitely going to stay out of trouble. Well ... we'll **try** to keep out of bad trouble.

Never forget that we're on a top-secret mission of vital importance to the nation. Well, we could be. It's totally vital that you never, ever, do the following things:

 Show anyone your mobile. In fact it's best if you leave it at home – it's not as if there's any reception here.

 Pay for something with the wrong money (see p. 24). That '2005' on your 10p piece is a dead giveaway.

 Say you'll look something up on the Internet!

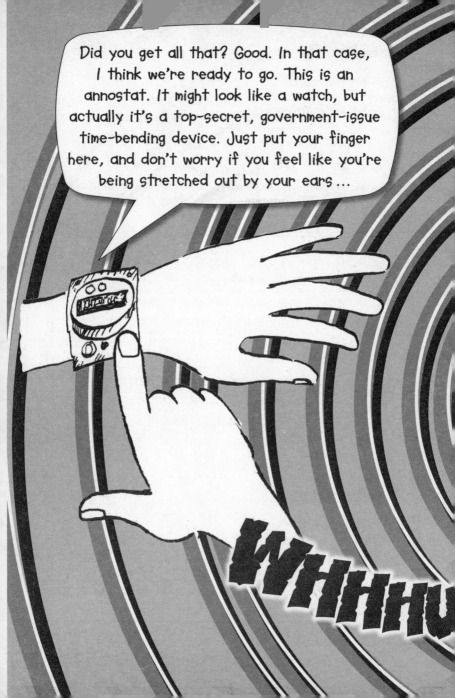

Oh, you noticed the smell, huh? You'll get used to it. It's mostly horse poo from all the traffic – that and smoke from fires. When you get closer to the river it gets much, much stronger. There's a lot worse than just dung floating around in there!

One vital thing to remember in Victorian London is to mind your step at all times, particularly when it's been raining. London mud is famously disgusting. It's grey, it's gloopy and it's everywhere. It's about 30% horse poo, 30% city dust and 40% dead rats, by the smell of it.

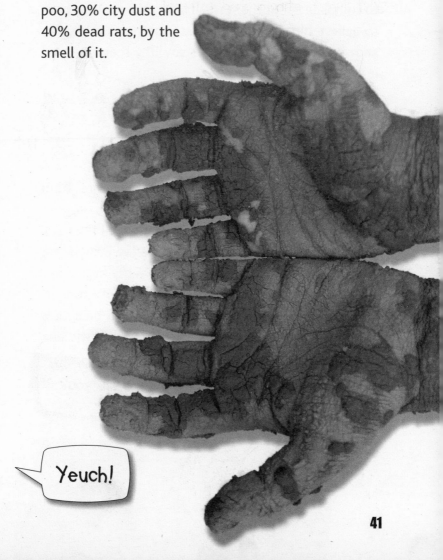

Yeuch!

And while you're watching out for the mud, remember you can't trust the water round here either. Mostly it's just like the mud, but a bit runnier.

One bloke in Yorkshire has written to the government to complain about the state of his local river. They have to believe him because the letter he sends is all grey and smelly – the river water's so filthy that he's used it as ink.

The Revenge of the Toilets

Most of London's drinking water still comes from the Thames. And most of London's sewage still goes straight into the Thames. Not to mention all the toxic goo that comes out of London's factories. Even if you find water from a well a long way from the river, don't assume it's safe to drink. Lots of toilets empty straight into big holes called cesspools. When the cesspools leak or overflow the sewage gets everywhere, including into the wells.

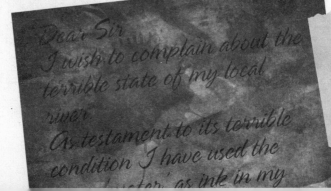

Dear Sir
I wish to complain about the terrible state of my local river.
As testament to its terrible condition I have used the water as ink in my

The government can't ignore the situation for much longer: the Great Stink is coming to get them. In 1858, there's going to be a super-hot, sweaty summer. It's going to make the river smell so bad, it'll make the MPs' eyes water in the Houses of Parliament. Clearly something must be done, so they build a massive network of proper sewers which will still be used right into the twenty-first century.

There's even air pollution back in 1851 too. Sure, there aren't any cars, but before electricity, everything runs on coal or oil. There's smoke and black soot everywhere, from factories, gasworks, steam trains, and fires in houses. I always get black bogeys when I stay here for a day or so.

The Dreaded Victorian Lurgy

Before travelling to Victorian London, History Spies should book themselves in for a course of vaccinations. There are lots of nasty diseases floating around, especially in the poor parts of town. Be extra careful about the water you drink – boil it first! And look out for the symptoms of any of these horrible plagues:

Typhoid fever

This is going to kill Prince Albert in 1861.

Symptoms: fever, headache, diarrhoea, a rash of red spots, swollen stomach

Avoid it: Typhoid is transmitted through dirty water or food. Watch what you drink and eat!

Typhus

Symptoms: headache, high fever, coughing, a rash which starts on the chest

Avoid it: Typhus is passed on by body lice, so keep yourself clean.

Cholera

Symptoms: severe diarrhoea, skin turns black and blue, death in a day or two

Avoid it: You catch cholera by drinking infected water, but most Victorians don't know that yet. ALWAYS boil water before you drink it to kill the germs.

Diphtheria
Symptoms: sore throat, swollen neck, fever, difficulty swallowing
Avoid it: Diphtheria is spread by touching an infected person, or breathing in their infected air.

Tuberculosis
The number one killer! Also known as 'TB'.
Symptoms: pale skin, chest pain, coughing up blood, red eyes, weight loss, exhaustion

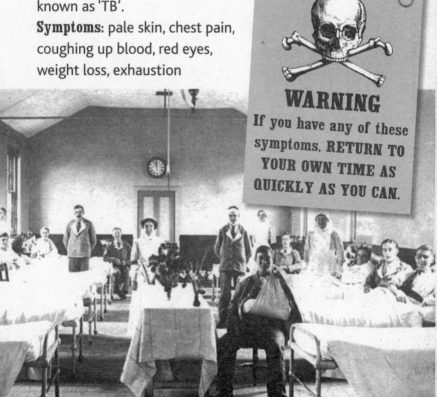

WARNING
If you have any of these symptoms, RETURN TO YOUR OWN TIME AS QUICKLY AS YOU CAN.

Avoid it: Get vaccinated, and avoid people with a bad cough.

There are some diseases you don't have to worry about:

Rickets

Symptoms: thin legs, bent out of shape

Avoid it: Rickets is caused by a bad diet without enough Vitamin D. You can't catch rickets, but you might see Victorian kids with it. Because of the modern diet and medicine, History Spies will find that they are clearly taller and bigger than Victorians of their own age.

People always think I'm at least a couple of years older when I'm here. It's great!

If you absolutely can't get home, you'll have to find treatment in 1851. This should be done extremely carefully.

Pharmacists

You can get pills made up in the pharmacist's for minor illnesses. It's safer than going to the doctor's, but watch out – they also sell hard drugs! Opium is like the dreadful modern drug heroin. It's legal and you can buy it at every high-street chemist's. People give it to their babies to stop them crying.

Surgeons

Watch out: surgery can be unhygienic and very painful. Firstly, you'll have to be awake for your operation. Pain-killing anaesthetics are only just being developed in 1851, and most surgeons still don't use them. Also there's no antiseptic until 1867, so you're very likely to catch an infection if you're operated on.

You can get really paranoid if you stop and think about all the germs – it's best if you just don't think about them, I reckon.

You have to be quite well off to have running water at home in 1851. Everyone else has to go out and get their water from a well, a standpipe or a river. Or if you don't have any of those handy, you can buy water from a water-carrier in the street. It costs a penny a bucket. It's safer just to drink tea or beer. If you do want a glass of water, remember that boiling water for several minutes before you drink it will kill most germs.

If you just want to wash in the water, you could try the public baths. They only cost a penny a go. Don't go too often though, or you'll look (and smell) funny. No normal Victorian has a bath every day. They don't think it's healthy to get wet all over. Some daring people take hip baths, where you sit in a shallow puddle of water and wash yourself carefully with a flannel.

Cows in the City

Before motorized refrigerated vans, it would take ages to get meat from farms to the city. The meat would be pretty green and maggoty by the time it got to London. So instead, farmers bring live animals right into the city.

Every Monday and Friday, the streets around Smithfield market are packed with live sheep, pigs and cattle. And squeezed in with them are the 'drovers' – the guys who bring them to market – and their dogs. Animals are everywhere. In 1851, a 'bull in a china shop' isn't just a figure of speech, it's an everyday worry.

Once all the animals are tied up in the market, they'll be sold and killed. The streets around Smithfield are full of slaughterhouses. Be careful not to slip on all the blood and guts.

Squeamish History Spies – and vegetarians – should avoid Smithfield on market days if possible. Even before they're killed, the animals here are treated badly. They're the main reason why the RSPCA was set up in 1824.

Well, that explains the noise. It's the sound of hundreds of pigs squealing, bulls bellowing, dogs barking and farmers yelling. Sounds a bit like my school at break.

Of course, people in London also need to buy fresh milk. If you've ever left milk out of the fridge for long you'll know how bad it must be in 1851. So all over the city, there are cows living in cellars so the neighbours can have farm-fresh milk.

Well, the good news is that this area's the best place to get meat for dinner. Speaking of which, I'm starving – fancy getting something to eat?

MR CAMPTON'S DELECTABLE PIES

Well, you can't go wrong with a nice pie, can you?

Pies of Peril

History Spies may already have heard of the devilish Victorian villain Sweeney Todd ('the Demon Barber of Fleet Street'). The story of Sweeney's been around for a few years, and you can go and see a play about him. In the story, Sweeney Todd is a barber who slits his customers' throats while he's shaving them. He then steals their money and valuables, and his neighbour Mrs Lovett cuts up their bodies and makes them into pies.

There's also a rumour going round that cheating shopkeepers are selling meat pies made of kittens. So far, there has been no evidence that this is a common problem. History Spies should also remember that Sweeney Todd is probably just a fictional character. Most pies in 1851 are safe to eat.

Yeah ... on second thoughts, I'm not that into pies. Come on, let's see what else we can find. This stall sells pea soup and hot eels ... bleurgh!

This is more like it – a fried fish shop. Victorians eat loads of fish. You're going to have to get used to herring.

It's quite nice, this, but it just makes me miss chips. Honestly – they've invented steam trains, gas lamps, photographs, even the telegraph – but no one's got around to inventing the chip yet. Rubbish!

Potatoes: the Dark Side

Back in 1845 some potato farmers in Ireland dug up their crop, only to find that they'd turned into a rotten black mush. For the next few years, this 'potato blight' destroyed almost all of the potatoes in Ireland. This was grim for the Irish people, because around half of them only had potatoes to eat. A million people died of hunger, and a million more left Ireland. So by 1851, there are a lot of Irish people living in London, and most of them are very poor.

Menu

There are definitely some top meals to be had if you've got the cash. Restaurants are a new fad in London, but you can get fancy food in gentlemen's clubs or if your rich friend asks you round for dinner. Sadly, I don't think any of the new restaurants are going to serve a couple of kids off the street.

Never mind, have a sweet. What do you fancy, hardbake or boney ribs?

Hardbake's a cheap kind of toffee, and Bonaparte's Ribs, or boney ribs, are a type of lollipop. That's better than hot eels, isn't it?

So, if the water's too dirty to drink, what can you have?

Thirsty Work

Tea is the most important drink in Victorian England. Everyone drinks tea all the time, even the poorest people who can't really afford food. History Spies should drink tea to fit in, but also because it's the safest drink available. Just make sure the water's definitely been boiled. And if you can, bring your own tea to make sure there aren't any added floor-sweepings in it.

The other drink everyone loves is beer. Pubs are a great place to spy on ordinary people. Pubs are more comfortable than most people's houses, so they spend a lot of time there. You'll find plenty of useful gossip down the pub, even if you're too young for beer. It's even the place people go to find out about jobs. There aren't any laws yet about children not going into pubs on their own, so even young History Spies can go in.

But I reckon, why go to a pub when you can go to a palace? Gin palaces are kind of like pubs, but so much cooler. People don't just go to get drunk, they go because of all the lights, the glass, the mirrors ... And because they hire pretty girls to serve the drinks. Even the drinks have glamorous names like 'The Celebrated Butter Gin'. I wonder if we could get one without the gin in it?

Shock! Horror!

ICE CREAM

Ice creams turned up in
London for the first time
last year, in 1850. They're
causing quite a sensation.
Londoners who'd never
eaten anything frozen before
tend to bite into their ice creams
and gobble them up too quickly.
It's funny watching people
hopping about clutching their jaws,
all confused because they've got
brain freeze and sensitive teeth!

Aha – a school. Come in here for a bit, I think you should see this. Don't worry, we won't stay long.

You're late! Come up here. Show me your hands. They're filthy! Where have you been?

Talk about bad luck. I hate school in 1851 more than school back home. It's pretty grim, and it's so **boring**. Well, I just hope you know your list of European capitals, because I certainly don't.

Like School, But Worse

Not all children in 1851 go to school. It's not against the law not to go. There are lots of children who have to work or beg on the streets instead, or whose parents can't afford to send them to school. Poor children can go to a charity school or ragged school, but they don't learn much more than a bit of reading and writing and some basic maths.

Even if you're pretending to be a rich kid, school won't be cushy. Young History Spies will need to do some serious revision if they plan to attend a private school in 1851. Well-off boys have to learn Latin and Greek at school, and if you don't make the grade, you'll find the teachers in Victorian schools can be very violent.

Even the classrooms look strict. The desks are all in neat rows, and talking in class will be severely punished. In very crowded schools, one teacher will teach a class of around 100 pupils, with older pupils helping. The teacher tells the older children what the lesson is, and they then teach it to the younger ones.

Even if you haven't always enjoyed lessons in your own time, you're bound to find 1851 school even less fun. There are no colourful books, no videos, no trying out experiments for yourself and definitely no games. In fact, fun is pretty much forbidden.

Instead, Victorian schoolchildren spend most of their time copying sentences from the blackboard. Older children will do this in an exercise book, younger children will just have a slate. You write on a slate using a sharp, pencil-shape piece of slate, and then wipe it clean again with a wet sponge or a good blob of spit. As a break from this, you can expect to learn facts parrot-fashion, by repeating after your teacher. You could be asked to name the countries of the world, or recite a list of historical dates.

As an exercise to prepare yourself for school in 1851, turn to page 134 of this guide. Learn as many of the dates as you can, in order, until you can say them out loud. If you can't manage, you'll make a lot of Victorian teachers very angry.

However bad school is for Victorians, there are some girls who would probably love to have the chance to get a proper education. People don't usually bother to send girls to school for very long. Some doctors even think that too much education makes girls ill. That could be because there aren't any women doctors until 1865.

Oh no, it's maths. This day is just going from bad to worse. I wish I had a calculator on me. Hey, do you know how to use an abacus?

How about your twelve times table? Don't worry, I think we're all going to get a chance to recite it...

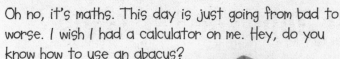

DING-DING!

DING-DING!

DING-DING!

Brilliant – lunchtime. Come on, let's get out of this dump!

Jobs for the Kids

If the prospect of going to school is just too horrible, why not try working instead? Kids often have to work in Victorian times, and there are all kinds of jobs going which can be useful to a young History Spy.

Errand boy

Hang around in the street looking trustworthy, and sooner or later someone will give you something to do. You can earn pennies by holding a gentleman's horse for him like a human parking meter, or by delivering a message for someone. And this can be a great excuse for skulking in the streets doing a bit of spying.

Chimney sweep

If you're small and thin, you could disguise yourself as a chimney sweep. You'll have to force your way up tiny brick chimneys, get covered in soot, and try very hard not to get stuck. You'll be glad to hear that there are less painful ways to get inside a house to spy on it.

Mudlark

Really poor kids scrape a living standing in the chilly river mud all day, looking for scraps of coal and anything valuable that's been dropped off the side of a boat. There aren't many spying jobs that make it worth pretending to be a mudlark.

Through the Keyhole

The role of 'domestic servant' is an especially handy one for a spy. There are more than a million servants working all over Britain in 1851, which means you can find a way into all kinds of homes. You can get great access to someone's house and their private life. Depending on your job, you can snoop around their business files, their kitchens, even their underwear drawers.

Servants also move around often, so that your sudden appearance and disappearance won't be too shocking. People come to London every day looking for work. Just apply for a job advertised in the newspaper, or register with a job agency or 'registry office'.

History Spies intending to get jobs as servants must arrange for fake references before they leave. Also be prepared for extremely hard work.

And be careful: employers can be suspicious of their servants. They may be watching you when you think you're spying on them!

Consider these disguises:

Pageboy

Dress: one old suit for dirty work, one smart suit for when you're on show

Main duties: running errands, cleaning boots

Spy-suitability: You get out of the house more than other servants do, which can be useful.

Nursemaid

Dress: plain dress, apron, cap, collar

Main duties: taking care of the children of the family

Spy-suitability: You can find out all about Victorian children, of course. But you can also get all the best gossip from the nearby families when you meet up with other nursemaids. You get to take the children for a walk in the park every day, so there are lots of chances for a chat.

Housemaid

Dress: dark dress, apron, cap

Main duties: cleaning the house, answering the door, keeping out of the way

Spy-suitability: You'll be almost invisible as a housemaid. You also get to wander all over the house, and if you're careful you can go through all sorts of cupboards and drawers. Only agents with good stamina should try this. Getting up at 5am to clean a house all day and then complete a spying mission can be exhausting.

I don't think we should get a job yet. My friend Lucy lives quite close, so let's go and see her instead. I should get her a present first, though. She likes reading – let's see what we can find.

Victorian Book Club

Ever heard of *Moby Dick?* It's a novel about a man called Captain Ahab who's obsessed with hunting a white whale, and it's first published this year.

A kids' book that's very popular this year is a fairy tale called *King of the Golden River*, by John Ruskin. It's all about how being kind and selfless can make you rich.

I'm not sure how that works exactly – I'm fairly sure it only happens in fairy stories.

Handily, you can now buy your books in a branch of WH Smith. This is the year when William Henry Smith starts a business selling books on the platforms of the Northwestern Railway, so that people will have something to read on the train. Turns out this is a pretty good business idea.

Breaking News

It's important that History Spies keep up with the latest news wherever they are. That's not as easy back in 1851 without the Internet, the TV or even the radio. You'll just have to go back to buying actual newspapers.

The Times is the most famous newspaper in London. Have a look at *The Illustrated London News* too – there aren't any photos in newspapers yet, but the *ILN* has hand-drawn pictures of all the most exciting news!

News is heading for London at a breakneck speed these days, thanks to a German bloke called Baron Julius Reuter. This year, he's setting up a high-tech link-up to Europe with the new-fangled electric telegraph, so that all the foreign news can get to London in a flash.

THE ILLUSTRATED LONDON NEWS

No. 1.]   FOR THE WEEK ENDING SATURDAY, MAY 14, 1842.   [SIXPENCE

MURDER!

If your spying cover is to pretend to be a poor person, you'll look odd reading *The Times* in public. Instead, try buying a chapbook from a seller in the street. They're like one-page newspapers, and the stories are almost always about grisly murders. You can also buy stories about criminals who've been executed, and find out what they said just before they were hanged. For something a bit jollier, you can even buy a news report on a horrible strangling which comes with its own song lyrics, so you can sing the gruesome story to all your friends.

Right, I've got what I was after – a really horrible song about the Murder in the Red Barn. Lucy will love it.

71

This is the maid's room up in the attic. It's a bit poky, but servants are used to that. She works so hard anyway, she doesn't get to spend much time in her room!
And here's the nursery where my brother Billy and I spend most of our time.

The Nursery

This is my brother Billy. I know he looks a bit like a girl – it's because he's only six so he hasn't been given his first pair of trousers yet! I have great fun teasing him.

You won't see any teddy bears – there's no such thing for at least another fifty years.

This is my diabolo – it's also called a 'devil on two sticks'. You put the diabolo on the string and make it spin around by moving the sticks about. With a bit of practice, you'll be able to throw it up in the air and catch it again.

Do you have a spinning top at home? They're really popular, but you have to practise if you want to spin them properly.

Top Toys

To practise your spinning-top technique and impress your Victorian friends, make yourself a top before you travel to 1851. Here are two types to choose from:

1) Basic. Can safely be taken to 1851 without arousing suspicion.

- Find a piece of card, a toothpick, some glue, and some crayons/paints/glitter.
- Cut a circle out of the piece of card and decorate it – spirals work well.
- Stick the toothpick carefully through the middle of the card.
- Spin!

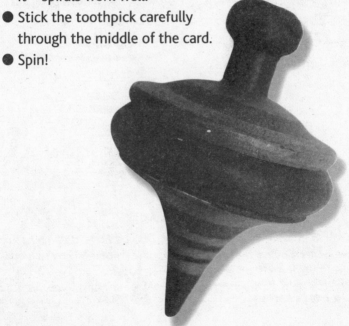

2) Modern. Looks prettier, but should not be taken to 1851 in case someone is too impressed and tries to find out what a CD is.

- Find a CD nobody minds you messing up, a marble, some strong glue, and a plastic pen cap.
- Glue the marble on to the non-shiny side of the CD, so that it balances in the hole.
- Glue the pencap on to the other side of the marble so that you can twizzle it.
- Spin!

Oh no, my mum's calling. We're going to have a sing-song. Thanks again for the present. Goodbye . . .

These boys are playing with wooden tops, which can give you a nasty knock!

I feel so sorry for Lucy. The only music she gets to listen to is her mum playing the piano, and she picks some useless songs.

Sing-a-Long-a-1851

History Spies with musical abilities will find themselves welcome in Victorian homes. Familiarize yourself with this popular song:

Home Sweet Home

This song was made famous by Jenny Lind, a singer nicknamed 'the Swedish nightingale'. The writer Hans Christian Andersen was in love with Jenny. He wanted to write a romantic story to express his love and he came up with . . . 'The Ugly Duckling'. Funnily enough, this didn't win her over.

Mid pleasures and palaces though we may roam,
Be it ever so humble there's no place like Home!
A charm from the skies seems to hallow us there,
Which seek thro' the world is ne'er met with elsewhere;

Home, Home, sweet, sweet Home,
There's no place like Home,
There's no place like Home.

Have you ever heard a more boring song in your life? And everyone loves it. Sometimes I get this urge to play some really loud hip-hop to a Victorian family to see if their heads explode.

Fun for All the Family

What on earth did Victorians do on quiet evenings in, with no telly, no Internet, no phones to chat to their friends...? If your mission requires you to spend time hanging out with respectable families, you can expect to while away the evenings doing one of these exciting activities:

Reading novels!
Playing card games!
Playing backgammon!
Playing the piano!
Putting on a show in a toy theatre!
Playing musical chairs!

> Some of that stuff sounds a bit boring, but it's fun if you're with your mates. And Victorians really know how to throw a Christmas party.

The Victorians invented many of the things you think of as Christmassy.

TREES: Prince Albert, Queen Victoria's German husband, made Christmas trees trendy in 1848. Don't get too close to a Victorian Christmas tree though – before electric fairy lights, they're covered in real candles!

CRACKERS: Invented in 1847. The snap inside a cracker is supposed to sound like a log crackling on a cosy open fire.

CARDS: The first Christmas cards in Britain were sent in 1843 and showed a cheery family having a drink. Pictures of robins and glittery snow came later.

CAROLS: The Victorians wrote some of our favourite Christmas carols. In 1851, you can belt out 'God Rest Ye Merry Gentlemen' or 'The Holly and the Ivy'. But if you start a chorus of 'Good King Wenceslas' or 'Away in a Manger', don't expect anyone to join in. They haven't been written yet.

SANTA CLAUS: The Victorians know about Father Christmas, but Santa Claus doesn't arrive in Britain until the 1860s. He's fat, jolly, and he flies round bringing children presents – pretty much as you know him today.

SCROOGE: Charles Dickens wrote *A Christmas Carol* in 1843. As well as the snow, the big family dinners, and the parties that we all like at Christmas, Dickens' story brought us the ultimate anti-Christmas meanie: Ebenezer Scrooge. Bah humbug!

It's nice visiting people in their homes, but sometimes it's more exciting to go for a wander round the streets. It's like an open-air circus all year round here! You can see jugglers, acrobats, dancing bears, and all kinds of musicians. There are bagpipers from Scotland, hurdy-gurdy men with dancing monkeys, guitar-players, drummers from South-East Asia...

...and this guy! We're in luck – meet the Amazing Sallementro!

Sallementro swallows stuff for a living. Stuff like knives, swords, and even SNAKES. Apparently the trick for sword-swallowing is to oil the sword first, and make sure you use a blunt one, of course! And for snakes, you have to take the stingers out. In fact, I don't recommend you try it at all. This guy says he couldn't eat for two months while he was learning, which doesn't sound like fun to me. Let's just watch the expert instead.

What's On

History Spies in search of entertainment are spoilt for choice in Victorian London. Try some of our highlights:

● Take in the latest **opera** in Covent Garden in your smartest evening dress. All the posh people like opera – it's much more trendy than going to the theatre.

● Head to a pub with a **music hall** attached for a less posh sort of concert. For sixpence you can listen to Victorian pop songs – and see acrobats if you're lucky.

● Gawp at some African bushmen or Mexican dwarfs, specially imported by a **showman**. Victorians will pay to have a look at people they find weird or interesting, especially 'freaks'. That includes people who are unusually tall, short or fat, as well as bearded ladies and people covered in tattoos. In the 1880s a young man called Joseph Merrick will become famous as 'the Elephant Man'. Joseph had an enormous head and a body bent out of shape, and frightened people who saw him. But after he found a home in the London Hospital, Joseph became a celebrity, and people started to see him as a normal person instead of a thing to stare at.

- Visit **London Zoo** in Regent's Park. The reptile house is still pretty new and exciting, and if your timing's good you could watch the boa constrictor squash a duck for its dinner!

- Be revolted by the **Chamber of Horrors** at Madame Tussaud's waxworks exhibition. You only need to travel back another year or two and you can meet the famous Madame herself!

- Nip into a **pub** in a poor part of town if you want to see something really horrible. Some pubs have rat pits, where you can watch dogs trying to catch rats, and the rats fighting back.

- Head to Astley's Amphitheatre in Lambeth for a real Victorian **circus** experience. As well as acrobats, jugglers and clowns, you'll see expert horse riders doing death-defying tricks. They even stage whole battles on horseback! The circus is huge in Victorian England. If he's in the country, try to catch a show by the American performer Richard Sands. His speciality is 'ceiling walking'. He walks upside-down on ceilings using special rubber suction pads on the soles of his shoes. Later, he'll die on stage in America when he tries to walk on a dodgy ceiling, grips hold of some loose plaster, and falls off.

- If you're missing the cinema, try a **diorama** instead. You sit in a darkened auditorium, just like at the movies, but instead of a screen there are two cloths with slightly different paintings on them. With clever lighting, the pictures switch from one to the other.

- Still not gripped by watching one picture change into another? How about a '**moving panorama**'? Go on a cruise down the Nile without leaving London – as someone unwinds a picture on a very long roll BEFORE YOUR VERY EYES!

Yeah ... they really do need television round here.

Messages from Beyond the Grave

Over in America, there's a bizarre new trend starting up. It's called spiritualism, where people communicate with the spirits of the dead.

It all started in 1848 with three young sisters called Kate, Leah and Maggie Fox, who live in a haunted house in New York State. Strange banging noises are heard in their house, and when they ask questions, the spirit answers them by rapping on the walls and floors.

The Fox sisters quickly become famous, and other people start trying to talk to the dead as well. Psychic mediums hold seances where they go into trances and contact spirits who answer questions from the audience. Some mediums claim to be able to produce a strange supernatural goo called ectoplasm from their mouths and nostrils!

The first medium comes to Britain in 1852, and very soon all the fashionable people are hosting 'table-

turning parties'. They sit in a circle round a table and wait for the spirits to make it tip up and spin around.

Forty years after she first heard from the ghost in her house, Maggie Fox finally owns up. She says the Fox sisters made the rapping noises themselves, by learning to crack the knuckles in their fingers and toes. But even though the Foxes' ghost was a hoax, spiritualism stayed popular and is still around in the twenty-first century.

Wow! That is one really effective practical joke! Imagine how embarrassed you'd be when everyone started believing you . . .

The Sports Section

Football

You can go and join in a football game in 1851, but you might not know what's going on. There aren't really any rules yet. Every village or school makes up its own rules – or doesn't bother with rules at all. Some places think it's OK to run with the ball, and fighting's allowed in some games. The Football Association won't be founded until 1863. After that you get referees who aren't completely confused.

Tennis

There's no tennis apart from 'real tennis' – which means 'royal tennis', not 'proper tennis'. It's played indoors with wonky rackets, and it makes absolutely no sense. Oh, and ladies can't play it at all. Someone has to invent lawn tennis later in the century, which is what you'd probably think of as 'proper tennis'.

> Of course, before people could play lawn tennis someone had to invent . . . the lawnmower!

Posh Pursuits

If you want to try a posh sport, you could get out of London and go shooting. Bagging a few pheasants and partridges for supper is a great way to impress your most important friends.

A Day at the Races

Everybody loves a bit of horse racing – watching it, of course, not doing it. On Derby Day, all kinds of people from toffee-nosed swells to scruffy nobodies make a day of it and have a flutter on the horses.

Pub Punch-ups

If you think Victorians are uptight and polite, check out a prize fight and prove yourself wrong! In pubs in the wrong part of town, burly blokes punch each other to win cash prizes.

Er ... do you mind if we skip this one? I think it sounds a bit risky.

Rowing

If you fancy a day out by the river, you can watch a rowing race on the Thames. It's not just the Oxford and Cambridge boat race – there are loads of races between watermen, the professionals who row ferries up and down the river.

NOT YET: The Olympics

Even though the Olympic Games started way back in Ancient Greece, there haven't been any for over 1,500 years. The modern Olympics don't start until 1896. So for now, the British can sit back and believe they're the best in the world at everything, without the risk of being beaten.

Let's try the opera, shall we? It's a bit of a walk to the nice part of town though.

What? . . . I said IT'S QUITE A LONG WAY!!

Victorian Traffic Jams

Just because there aren't any cars or lorries in 1851, it doesn't mean the streets are empty and filled with the gentle sound of birdsong. The streets of London are packed with carts, carriages, taxis, buses . . . All the traffic going anywhere south-east of London crosses over London Bridge. There are traffic jams all over the city. And when horses get stuck in a traffic jam, they make sure you know about it. Apart from all the animals and the shouting, the roads themselves are noisy. They aren't covered in tarmac – they're made of stone. If you want to imagine the noise iron carriage wheels make going over stone roads, try running a big stick along some metal railings. Now multiply that noise by ten and add in all those horses' hoofs. When the car is finally invented, people are delighted. They think it's going to get so much quieter when everyone's using those new-fangled rubber wheels!

Dark Alleys

History Spies should take great care going out after dark in Victorian London. The gas lamps in the streets aren't as bright as twenty-first-century street lights. Gas flames are fan-shaped, smoky, and yellow in colour. You'll also notice they have a slightly funny smell. So far, the streets and homes of the richer people are lit by gas. There's no such thing as an electric light bulb yet. Ordinary people still use candles, or lamps which sometimes burn oil from sperm whales.

Because of all the thick black smoke in London, the backstreets can be pretty dingy even in the daytime. Some shops have to keep the gas lights on all day because there's not enough light from outside.

I mean, you're OK cos you're with me, right? But if you weren't... Well, let's just say the streets aren't that safe round here. You'll want to look out for some of these scary bad guys:

APPEAL FOR INFORMATION:

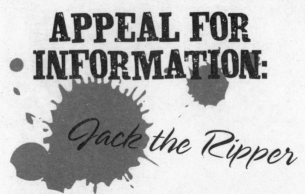

Jack the Ripper

Jack the Ripper was one of history's most famous serial killers – but no one has any idea who he was.

In the autumn of 1888, a string of women were found horribly murdered in the East End of London. They'd had their throats cut and their bodies 'ripped' open. The murderer got his nickname after someone sent a letter to the police, signed 'Jack the Ripper'. We still don't know if it was really from the murderer, or just a prank.

There was a huge police hunt and all sorts of crazy ideas about who the killer might be. A doctor? A vicar? A woman? The truth is, we still don't have a clue who did it.

The Bizarre Case of Spring-Heeled Jack

Another 'Jack' first turned up a few years ago, in the 1830s. Witnesses say he's a tall figure wrapped in a

cloak, wearing a white oilskin (waterproof) costume with a big helmet on his head, and carrying a lantern. Apparently he can also jump great heights, as if he has springs in his shoes.

One of Jack's victims, Jane Alsop, answered a loud knocking at her door. She told the police that 'With one bound he was in front of her, and before she had a chance to move, he belched blue flames from his mouth into her face.' He then grabbed her and started tearing her clothes with his sharp metal claws.

Of course, Jane could have made him up, or she could have been seeing things. But plenty of other people have seen Spring-Heeled Jack bouncing around and spewing fire. Some of them have also seen his steely claws and his tight white outfit.

Any History Spies encountering Spring-Heeled Jack should attempt to gather as much information as possible. Photographs, activity reports, fingerprints and hair or blood samples which could be used to extract DNA could all be vital evidence in this mysterious case.

Who was Jack? It's still a complete mystery. Maybe he really was a monster, or perhaps an alien, a demon or a ghost. Probably he was someone dressed up, but what was he dressed *as*? Why would you pick claws, springy shoes and firebreathing as your super-powers?

You meet some proper oddballs in Victorian London, I'm telling you.

Dastardly Victorian Villains

Baby-farmers

If someone in 1851 has a baby they can't or don't want to keep, they can pay a baby-farmer to look after it. Baby-farms may sound like places where toddlers get to play with cute little lambs, but they're more like prisons. Babies are kept alive on as little food as possible, so the people 'looking after' them get to keep plenty of leftover cash. Running a baby farm isn't illegal, but some baby-farmers are definitely criminal. Some will take money from a mother to look after her baby, and then fill its bottle with gin so it sleeps all day.

Toy-getters

A 'toy-getter' is slang for a thief who steals watches. Watches are very expensive in 1851 and you don't wear them on your wrist, you keep them in your pocket dangling from a chain. A gold watch and chain are tempting to thieves. People try all kinds of things to keep their watches safe, from hard-to-reach pockets to thief-proof chains, but desperate pickpockets are still hard at work in the streets of London. History Spies should keep their wits about them at all times and keep valuables in a very safe place.

Skinners

Skinners are women who start talking to children in the street, get them to come around a corner, and then . . . no, they don't skin them. They steal their clothes. Clothes are expensive in 1851, and if you get a rich kid, you can make a lot of money from their fancy threads. So if you see a child wandering around in its underwear and crying, you'll know there's a skinner on the loose.

Dog thieves

While some criminals are concentrating on watches, others specialize in pinching pets. Fancy dogs are kidnapped to get money out of their rich owners. Scruffier mongrels are stolen for their skins, to make coats for people who'd like mink but can't afford it.

Wow! So 101 Dalmatians was a true story then?

Garrotte-men

At least toy-getters aren't usually violent. Watch out for a spate of garrottings going on in 1851. A garrotting is a robbery, with strangulation as an added extra. A well-dressed gent will be walking down the street when suddenly someone comes up behind him and grabs him around the throat. Then a second thief goes through his pockets. They take his money, valuables, and even his fancy clothes. Sometimes the 'thug' or garrotter will use a rope to strangle the victim during the attack. Any agent walking after dark should have some kind of weapon handy in case they meet this kind of criminal.

Cartoon from Punch magazine, 1856: wear an Antigarotte Collar ('elegantly studded with the sharpest spikes') to avoid being strangled!

Say It with Flowers

Every History Spy should be familiar with several code languages. The Victorians have made up a few especially odd ones of their own. Take the Language of Flowers, for

instance. It's sort of a game — a way for couples to send each other messages without getting caught.

Because it's based on flowers, most of the meanings are soppy things like 'true love' (a forget-me-not) or 'faithfulness' (blue violet). You can send serious messages with flowers too, though. You could warn someone to 'take care' with an azalea, or wish someone 'courage' by giving them some garlic.

Watch out for the following flowers:

Hellebore – scandal

Nightshade – dark thoughts

Cypress – death

Monkshood – deception OR danger is near

The Great Exhibition of the Industry of All Nations

I've never been to the Great Exhibition before, but I've heard about it. You've heard of Crystal Palace, right? The place? The football team? Well, there used to be a real Crystal Palace, and **this** is it.

Yup, here in Hyde Park is a whacking great hall made out of glass and iron. The Victorians decided to build the most impressive building they could, and stick their favourite things from all over the world inside it. It's their way of saying: 'Look at us! We're amazing! We've got all the stuff you could ever want to see!'

The Crystal Palace is six times bigger than St Paul's Cathedral, or the size of fifteen football pitches. It's so high that there are trees growing in the refreshment areas. Instead of cutting down the trees that were standing in the park, the builders just built around them.

I chose the best day of all to bring you here – 1 May 1851, the grand opening of the Great Exhibition. This is what I call a day out! You've got a brass band, a 600-person choir, organ music, sunshine, cheering crowds ... And best of all, let me introduce you to a BIG celebrity. Actually, she's a very short celebrity, but she's the most famous person you'll meet this century. Just over there – Her Majesty, Queen Victoria!

Queen Victoria – Action Hero!

She may look regal and a bit mumsy, but being Queen is a serious business and Vicky's got to be tough. When she's not opening exhibitions or posing with her babies, the Queen spends a lot of time dodging bullets.

She's already survived five people trying to assassinate her, and she's got another two attempts to go! She gets shot at so often, she owns a bullet-proof parasol.

Now, that is cool. Do you think I'd look silly if I carried a parasol?

Thirty thousand people cram into the Crystal Palace, and more than half a million settle for hanging around in Hyde Park trying to get a glimpse of Her Maj. There are lots of policemen and soldiers around, because there've been a few revolutions in Europe recently. People worry the Queen will be attacked.

Everyone's excited to be a Victorian. Great Britain is called 'the workshop of the world'. We make more than half of all the cotton cloth in the whole world, and it's made us very rich. Everyone is feeling pretty pleased with themselves for having made so much money from their hard work.

Maybe that's why there's this funny-looking sculpture at the entrance to the Crystal Palace. It's a whopping great lump of coal that weighs 24 tons. I guess you could run a lot of trains with that.

All Together Now

The Great Exhibition is a big success. In the six months it's open, six million people pay to look around. It makes enough money to pay for the opening of the Victoria and Albert Museum, the Royal Albert Hall *and* the Natural History Museum. People come from all over the country, and special trains run to take Exhibition visitors to London and back. It's an exciting journey for lots of people who haven't seen the big city before, and it just shows how much the railways have changed the world. Because people are flocking from all over the world, London is packed in 1851. For History Spies, this is useful: there are so many strange-looking people coming to town that it's easy to go unnoticed. You'll find lots of people keen to let out rooms to visitors.

Well, come on then! Let's have a look around. I want to see the stuffed elephant. Here, have a look at the list.

Here are just some of the *hundred thousand* awesome treasures and astounding inventions on show at the Great Exhibition:

● **The Koh-i-Noor Diamond**
All the way from the Punjab, this beautiful 105-carat diamond is displayed in a strong golden cage, and lit up by gaslight so that it really sparkles.

● **Food in Tins**
This amazing new invention preserves food for years! The inventor hopes that one day, tinned tomatoes will be available all across the land.

● **Stuffed Elephant**
Marvel at the gorgeous embroidery on the elephant's saddle and headdress. Come face to face with this magnificent animal in the Indian part of the exhibition. (This elephant is on loan from the Saffron Walden Museum as the Indians didn't send one.)

● Glass Eyes

One-eyed gentlemen will no longer have to suffer cruel stares. With these magnificent glass eyes, they can look like everyone else – it still won't help them see, though.

● A Stoat Tea Party

This charming group of real stuffed stoats is all dressed up and arranged at a tea table.

This is the freakiest thing I've seen in a while. Why would you do that to a dead stoat? I don't get it.

● **Alarm Bed**
Never be late
for work again, with this mechanical bed that folds
up and throws you out to make sure you get up on
time. Also, make time to see the bed that turns into
a life raft.

● **Celebrity Soap**
This bar of soap has been used by Jenny Lind. (Remember
her? Back on p. 77.)

● **Rhubarb Champagne**
Undoubtedly set to become the Drink of the Future!

● **The Liverpool Docks**
Just a model of course, but fully equipped with 1,600
tiny ships complete with rigging.

● **Musical Boxes**
All the way from Switzerland, these tiny ingenious
boxes play a tune without musicians.

● Dr Merryweather's Tempest Prognosticator

This magnificent gold cage is home to twelve leeches, each in a little glass jar. When the weather's going to be stormy, the leeches climb to the top of their jars, making a bell ring. This gadget may look good, but it's also a scientific way to avoid being struck by lightning!

● The Machine Gallery This

is everyone's favourite part of the Great Exhibition. It houses all the biggest, noisiest and most powerful machines there are. Come and see the steam locomotives, the huge steam hammer, the hydraulic presses . . .

● Envelope-folding Machine

When worked by two children, this gadget can make sixty envelopes a minute. Now that's progress.

● The Lord of the Isles

This massive steam locomotive weighs 31 tons!

● The Electric Telegraph

It sends messages to Edinburgh and Manchester in only a few minutes!

(Almost) Instant Messaging

The telegraph is an amazing new piece of technology in 1851. Just a few years ago, if you wanted to speak to someone you had to go and see them or send them a letter in the post, which could take days or even weeks. But in 1841, the first public telegraph office opened at Paddington station. For a shilling a go, you could send a message along the railway line to Birmingham and it only takes minutes! Soon, there are telegraph wires along all the railway lines, and in 1851 you can send a telegraph to most cities in Britain. It's still exciting though, and not everyone knows how to do it. When Queen Victoria sends telegraph messages at the Great Exhibition, people are impressed. Believe it or not, this big clanking machine is an ancestor of the text message.

WE R NOT MUZD :(

QV LOVES PA 4 EVA

I know some old people in the twenty-first century who can't send texts. That Queen Victoria was really advanced.

Crime-fighting Gadgets

John Tawell became famous in 1845. He was the first person ever to be arrested by telegraph. He murdered his wife in Slough, and then tried to escape on the train to London. But the Slough stationmaster sent a telegraph to Paddington station, telling them to arrest the man dressed as a Quaker who was sitting in the last compartment of the second first-class carriage. When he got to London, Tawell was followed by the police and then arrested.

This was a great advert for how useful the telegraph could be.

Wow! Just think how excited everyone here would be if you told them about the Internet — well, either that or they'd think you were mad. I think you'd better not mention it. Just act impressed, Ok?

Incredible Inventions

Coming here, you'd think that everyone in Britain had been busy inventing things and building gadgets for the last ten years. Actually, a lot of them have.

Steam power is the biggest news in science in 1851. This is the 'Age of Steam', and everything's running on steam, from trains to printing presses. To make steam, you need a lot of coal, so the mines are doing a roaring trade.

Electricity has been discovered, but it's not used for much yet. Michael Faraday made lots of important discoveries a few years ago, like how to generate electricity and how to get an electric motor to work. But it's when the light bulb is invented in 1878 that people really start to see what electricity can do.

Hold Really, Really Still ...

Photography is just getting started. It's been around since 1839, and there are lots of different kinds of cameras and film. All the cameras are big and heavy – you can't just take a few snaps at your friend's birthday party, you have to get a professional photographer to come round and do a proper photo session.

It won't be fun. Each picture takes several minutes to take and you have to stay very still for the whole time, otherwise they end up a blurry mess. In 1851 there's a

new kind of photography invented called the 'wet-plate process'. It does speed things up a bit – now, instead of a few minutes, each photo takes just fifteen seconds. But still, try it. Go and find a mirror and try holding a pose totally still while you count to fifteen in your head. If you've tried to stay smiling, you must look a bit weird by now. That's why everyone looks so glum in Victorian photos. They're bored out of their minds and concentrating really hard on not moving.

I think I may be stuck like this!

And if you stick around after 1851, there are some exciting scientific breakthroughs coming up ...

- In 1856, the first artificial dye for clothes is invented by accident. It's purple. Everyone goes mad for the bright-coloured clothes they can now afford. So many people wear purple, it's called the 'Mauve Age'.

- Charles Darwin's theory of natural selection is really going to start some fights when he publishes it in 1859. Lots of people will be very upset to be told they're descended from apes!

- The 'Electrical Speaking Telephone' will be invented by Alexander Graham Bell in 1876.

Sounds a lot more useful than the Electrical Humming Telephone, at least.

- In 1878 Sir Thomas Swan (in England) and Thomas Edison (in the USA) invent the electric light bulb at the same time. JINX!

- The first 'safety bicycles' are made in Coventry in 1886. Finally, a bike that fits in a bike shed!

- The radio will be patented by Guglielmo Marconi in 1896. Now pointless radio phone-in shows are just around the corner!

Dodgy Dinosaurs

Dinosaurs were only discovered in 1818, so studying them is a new and exciting science. Be careful what you say though. You almost certainly know too much about dino science, even if you only know what you saw in *Jurassic Park*.

At the end of 1851, the Great Exhibition closes down and the Crystal Palace is packed up and shifted to a big new park in Sydenham. To liven up the park, the owners get a sculptor to make massive model dinosaurs to hang out in the lakes and lurk between the trees. The sculptor, Benjamin Waterhouse Hawkins, throws himself into

his work and builds enormous life-size models. They're so big that on New Year's Eve, 1853, he gives a dinner party for twenty people *inside* the Iguanodon model! As you can imagine, everyone is terribly impressed and excited to see these extinct monsters up close for the first time.

It's a shame, then, that the models are almost totally wrong. Because people haven't been studying dinos for very long, they're making all kinds of silly mistakes. The Megalosaurus is standing on four legs, not two, and the Iguanodon has a horn on its head which shouldn't be there. Someone's stuck an Iguanodon skeleton together in the wrong shape – the 'horn' should actually be its thumb. And nobody's even heard of Tyrannosaurus rex, Diplodocus or Stegosaurus yet.

The Exhibition isn't just about gawping at shiny gadgets. It's supposed to bring about world peace. *The Times* says this is 'the first morning since the creation of the world that all peoples have assembled from all parts of the world and done a common act.'

They think if everyone comes and meets up in a big greenhouse, they're bound to get along and stop fighting. Obviously, not everyone who's come to the Exhibition is going to rush home and make sure there won't be any more wars. Would have been nice though, wouldn't it?

It's a Wonderful World

The Great Exhibition is especially exciting because it brings together inventions and art from all over the world. Not many people have ever been outside England before. They think it's amazing to see all these people and things from India, China and America.

The world is big and unknown back in 1851. There are no aeroplanes to take you to Timbuktu in a few hours, and there are huge parts of Australia and America that people in Britain have no idea about, because no one's been there yet. We've still got more than twenty years to go before the French writer Jules Verne writes *Around the World in Eighty Days* – something which seems completely impossible in 1851.

Lots of Victorians go off exploring on adventures into unknown jungles and deserts to find out more about the world. Some come back as heroes, others don't come back at all.

Cool – I've always wanted to be an explorer. And back in 1851, there was still stuff to discover! I want to be like all of these guys . . .

Intrepid Explorer Chaps

1) Edward Whymper

Edward will grow up to climb mountains all over the world – but he's only eleven in 1851. He says later:

'I had ideas floating in my head that I should one day turn out some great person, be *the* great person of *my* day, perhaps Prime Minister, or at least a millionaire.'

Yes! That's exactly how I feel!

2) Richard Burton

Richard started out in the Indian Army where he quickly learned seven languages – eventually, he'll learn to speak over forty. In 1853, he's going to make a death-defying expedition – he'll disguise himself as a sheikh and make the Muslim pilgrimage to Mecca, where no non-Muslims are allowed.

> He would have been a brilliant History Spy, this one.

3) Robert McClure

Robert is in Canada in 1851. He's trying to find the 'Northwest Passage', which is a way to get a boat through the Arctic ice. His expedition left in January 1850 and until 1853, no one at home knows what's happened to them. Before radios, it's easy for ships to just disappear.

4) Ludwig Leichhardt

Ludwig is missing in Australia right now. He hasn't been seen for three years. By 1851 he could be dead,

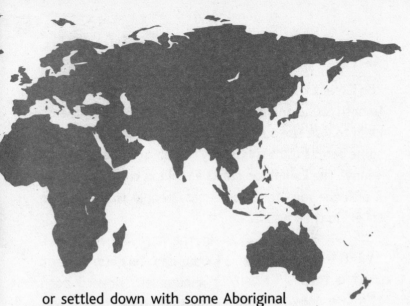

or settled down with some Aboriginal mates, or still wandering around lost.
People will try to search for him for years afterwards, but he never turns up.

5) David Livingstone

David spends his time exploring, telling Africans about Christianity, and getting into trouble. In 1843 he was savaged by a lion. He escaped with his life, but his arm hasn't been the same since. In August 1851 he discovers the Zambezi River, and in a few years he'll find a way to travel right across Africa.

Hmm. It does sound tough. But I still reckon I wouldn't be one of the ones that got lost!

Take a Break

The Great Exhibition is enormous, and you can't expect to dash round and see everything at once. You'll at least need to visit the public loos. They cost a penny to use — some people think this is why we talk about 'spending a penny'. The Exhibition starts a real loo craze. After this, it's all the rage for middle-class people to get indoor toilets in their houses.

> What's so exciting about a toilet, though? It's the jelly and ice cream I'm after.

In the refreshment areas, you can buy ice cream, lemonade, ginger beer, sausage rolls, bread and butter, and pies. Visitors to the Exhibition put away a total of 28,046 sausage rolls! You can eat your snacks under the indoor trees, or by the giant glass fountain which is over eight metres high.

> Well, it's time we were getting back, I think. Just a — Where is it?

Oh, I don't believe it! My annostat – I must have dropped it somewhere! Hang on. I know – quick, back to the machine gallery!

This is very, very bad news. If we don't get this back we're stuck here, and if they work out how to use it there'll be Victorians popping up all over history and we'll be in **so** much trouble.

129

The Time Map

This chart will help History Spies to avoid gaffes like using the phone in 1860, or showing someone a photo in 1830.

Metropolitan Police Act – the first paid uniformed police force in the country is set up. **1829**

Cholera reaches England from the East. **1832**

William IV dies. Victoria gets to be Queen. **1837**

The 'Chartists' start political riots. **1839**

Two inventors, Louis Jacques Daguerre and William Henry Fox Talbot, both have brilliant ideas. They call their inventions the 'daguerrotype', and the 'calotype', and they're both early kinds of photograph.

A Royal Wedding: Queen Victoria marries Prince Albert of Saxe-Coburg-Gotha. **1840**

1840	The Penny Post begins, meaning there's now no excuse for slackness with thank-you letters.
1841	Richard Owen invents the term dinosaur, which means 'terrible lizard'.
1842	Nelson's Column is built. Two minutes later, a historic pigeon is the first ever to poop on it.
1843	People start sending each other Christmas cards.
1844–5	Railway Mania – 5,000 miles of track built.
1845	The potato crop fails in Ireland, beginning the Great Famine.
1848–9	Cholera epidemic hits London.
1851	The Great Exhibition in London.

Spiritualism (the belief that people can talk to the spirits of the dead) arrives in England. And you thought the Victorians were so sensible and scientific!	**1852**
Frenchman Charles Gerhardt invents aspirin, but doesn't work out what the point of it is.	**1853**
Crimean War, where Britain fights against Russia in the Middle East. The Crimean War is Florence Nightingale's big break as a nurse.	**1854–6**
Sir William Perkin has an accident in his chemistry lab and invents a purple artificial dye. Everyone starts wearing mauve.	**1856**
The sentence of transportation to Australia for criminals is abolished.	**1857**
The Second Opium War opens up China to European trade.	**1857–8**
The Indian Mutiny.	**1858**
Summer: the Great Stink in London.	

1859   Publication of Darwin's
*On The Origin of Species Through
Natural Selection.* Everyone gets
very het up about the idea that
people are descended
from monkeys.

1860   Battersea Dogs' Home is founded.

1861   Prince Albert dies – Queen Victoria
starts wearing black.

1863   Steam-powered trains start
running on the Metropolitan
Line, the first line of the London
Underground.

Football Association founded –
now everyone has to play to the
same rules.

1865   Elizabeth Garrett Anderson
becomes the first woman doctor
in Britain.

Joseph Lister starts using carbolic
acid as disinfectant in surgery. It
cuts his patients' deaths by a third.

Alfred Nobel invents dynamite. **1866**

The last ever convict ship leaves for Western Australia. **1867**

Bank Holiday Act: everyone gets occasional Mondays off to go to the seaside. **1870**

Alexander Graham Bell invents the 'Electrical Speaking Telephone'. **1876**

Shampoo's invented in England. **1877**

Sir Theophilus Shepstone grabs the South African Republic for the British.

Sir Thomas Swan (England) and Thomas Edison (USA) invent the electric light bulb at the same time. JINX! **1878**

Zulu War between the British and the Zulus in South Africa. The Zulus lose. **1879**

1880	For the first time, it's made compulsory to go to school until you're ten years old.
1883	Gottlieb Daimler invents the internal combustion engine, which makes cars possible.
1886	Gold is discovered in the Transvaal in South Africa.
	The first 'safety bicycles' are manufactured at Coventry.
1888	'Jack the Ripper' commits grisly murders in Whitechapel, London.
1896	First regular cinema shows in London, at the Empire Theatre in Leicester Square.
	Italian inventor Guglielmo Marconi shows up in London with a 'wireless' – an early kind of radio.
1899	Aspirin is invented – properly, this time.
1901	Victoria dies, and her son Edward VII becomes King.

ESCAPE FROM VESUVIUS

HISTORY SPIES

Have you ever been on a top-secret, life-and-death, time-bending government mission before?

Pompeii: AD 79

Vesuvius is about to erupt and the Department of Historical Accuracy needs a History Spy with nerves of steel . . .

Your mission: find out what went on at a gladiator battle, why it's OK to burp at a banquet and why everyone in Pompeii was so smelly! Then, if you're brave enough, you can check out the eruption that buried the city for 2,000 years.

Join top History Spy Charlie Cartwright in his adventures as he travels through space and time, dodging bombs, dinosaurs and erupting volcanoes.

Have you ever been on a top-secret, life-and-death, time-bending government mission before?

Liverpool: 1940

The war is raging and the Department of Historical Accuracy need a brave and daring History Spy to uncover the truth...

Your mission: learn how to identify enemy aircraft, make spitfires out of saucepans and disguise yourself as an evacuee. Find out how people spoke, what they ate, and become a champion at marbles!

Join top History Spy Charlie Cartwright in his adventures as he travels through space and time, dodging bombs, dinosaurs and erupting volcanoes.

A selected list of titles available from Macmillan Children's Books

The prices shown below are correct at the time of going to press. However, Macmillan Publishers reserves the right to show new retail prices on covers, which may differ from those previously advertised.

All Pan Macmillan titles can be ordered from our website, www.panmacmillan.com, or from your local bookshop and are also available by post from:

Bookpost, PO Box 29, Douglas, Isle of Man IM99 1BQ

Credit cards accepted. For details:
Telephone: 01624 677237
Fax: 01624 670923
Email: bookshop@enterprise.net
www.bookpost.co.uk

Free postage and packing in the United Kingdom